Ridge Music

Ridge Music

Poems by Harry Humes

The University of Arkansas Press
Fayetteville   1987

DESIGNER: Chiquita Babb
TYPEFACE: Linotron 202 Goudy Old Style
TYPESETTER: G&S Typesetters, Inc.
PRINTER: McNaughton & Gunn, Inc.

The paper used in this publication meets the minimum require-
ments of the American National Standard for Permanence of
Paper for Printed Library Materials z39.48-1984. ∞™

LIBRARY OF CONGRESS CATALOGING-IN-PUBLICATION DATA

Humes, Harry.
    Ridge music.
    I. Title
PS3558.U444R5   1987   811'.54   87-6023
ISBN 0-938626-97-3
ISBN 0-938626-98-1 (pbk.)

For my wife Nancy,
and my daughters Rachel and Leah

Acknowledgments

Grateful acknowledgment is made to the following publications in which some of the poems in Ridge Music originally appeared: *Antaeus*, "So the River Goes"; *The Bellingham Review*, "The Last Miner is Found"; *Beloit Poetry Journal*, "Baking Bread During a Drought"; *Cincinnati Poetry Review*, "One Approach To the Steppes," "On Not Fishing the Brodhead This Year"; *Cumberland Poetry Review*, "The Man Who Loved Fish"; *CutBank*, "Mountain Lake with Stumps," "Listening to One Thing at a Time," "Winter Storm Watch"; *Kansas Quarterly*, "The Sermon Stump"; *Kayak*, "Entrails"; *Little Magazine*, "Swimming with Foxes," "The Christian Woman and Sasquatch," "Releasing the Minnows"; *Massachusetts Review*, "Building a Tower"; *Midwest Arts and Literature*, "The Photograph"; *Poet Lore*, "White Birch Father"; *Poetry Miscellany*, "The Man Who Smuggled Life to Work Day after Day"; *Poetry Northwest*, "Calling in the Hawk," "Ridge Music," "The Snow Snake"; *Raccoon*, "At the Shad Festival"; *Salmagundi*, "The Long Habit of Fire," "Waiting at the Crow Roost, He Thinks of the Woman Who Went Back to the City"; *Slackwater Review*, "To my Brother This Night on the Delaware River"; *West Branch*, "Improvements on Empty Space," "Bee Hive in Early December," "Caught in the Woods in the Dark."

"The Last Miner is Found" appears in a limited edition book, *Robbing The Pillars*, © 1984, Adastra Press, Easthampton, MA.

"The Man Who Loved Fish," "The Long Habit of Fire," and "So the River Goes" appear in a limited edition book, *Throwing Away the Compass*, © 1986, Silverfish Review, Eugene, OR.

"Calling in the Hawk" was awarded the Theodore Roethke Prize in 1984 by *Poetry Northwest*.

The final lines of "Words for the End of a Pond" are dedicated to John Cheever and his story "Goodbye, My Brother."

I wish to express my gratitude to the Pennsylvania Council on the Arts for Literary Fellowships in 1984 and 1986 that helped me complete this book.

I would also like to thank those who looked at these poems in their various stages: Nancy Humes, Jonathan Holden, Richard Savage, Kelly Cherry, William Pitt Root, and especially Miller Williams whose close reading and suggestions helped tremendously in giving Ridge Music its final shape.

Contents

Ridge Music

Entrails

Wait, something in the grass says,
as I come out of a green tunnel
of apple trees grown together like old dreams,
says the years pile up, curl away,
the sun grown too familiar,
old prophesying sounding as only
old guts in the grass can.

Says all of it as if it knows,
though when I look at the long string
of intestines winding under blue flies,
I know that earlier
a hunter had waited like rock
beside a groundhog's den.
So it is a day with blood in it,
and in it too the sharp click of a knife
and flesh opening with no sound at all.

I stand as still as that hunter
and think of what might come of such
slow burning and what distance rises
from such red shreds of death.
I can feel in all of it the tight hold
the coming dark has on everything.

In the flat light the guts grow flatter,
more difficult to understand.
Tomorrow after a night of mice
and slow feasting opossums, they'll be gone,
and grass might say nothing more for years.

Baking Bread During a Drought

This morning it was the quail flushing
near the almost dry pond that made me think
of small loaves of brown bread.

Now it is dark.
The countryside rises on moonlight.
I listen near the porch to windbells,
my neighbor's cows over the night's crust.

And measure flour
as I think of quail in their dusty circle
in the grass of the high field,
break open packages of yeast,
follow white silence between mix bowl
and table, wait for my life to double,
for my well to rise, the oven to pre-heat,
earth to grow soft with woodrot,
for crow blood to drizzle down.

Near midnight
when the news is dry as ever,
I go round with neither pity nor impatience
but with bread dance, rain dance,
dance of wife and child, all the moves
I try to remember in a season
shrinking beneath me inch by inch.

Words for the End of a Pond

Now it is over.
Bulldozer and backhoe have gone back
across timothy and alfalfa.
Your sons walk over the soft earth
to the marshy circle a foot across
and think of fish.

It is not mentioned at supper
nor later in the wooden chairs on the porch
how starlight no longer shatters
on the wings of dragonflies,
how the deer have wandered away.

Nor do you say ever
how as you slept there came a slow schooling
of eyes and dark backs near the bed,
and a wet wind dimpling the shallow sheets
and a popping of small mouths near the window.

Even the prayers you remembered
did not help, nor thinking of the buoyant breasts
of women, nor the narrow road curving into the hills.

Only the rustling of weeds
and something standing in moonlight.

Think how for years and years
as you walk through town or drink with friends
you will remember that night
swirling near the eye's dry corner
or in the bead along the side of the glass,
the way it all froze and thawed and froze
and spread out like a season
behind the muskrat's head.

How you will never forget the heron's cry
above the woman who once walked toward you
shining and naked from the pond.

So the River Goes

I am on a bridge.
It makes no difference where.
It could be winter,

late afternoon and gray,
so gray your heart forgets
its fool blood in the wings.

Hardly anything is moving.
A cold day of sad streets.
I have been thinking of my bones,

of how they look like buildings,
towers in a bell wind.
At least I have not dreamed of fish.

This river, though,
goes straight on south. Something hurts.
Could be the day or the lack of jokes.

Could be this frozen land
of swamp and wilderness. South!
A hot knocking at my soul.

Someone's passing, a stranger.
Before he's gone, call to him, wave.
If I'm lucky I could make it
to the Delta by early spring.

Releasing the Minnows

Here in the motionless canoe
it is all so familiar,
the way my knife slits the bellies
of bass, how I pull out entrails,
wash the cavities, or think
of ripe tomatoes, the way I take up bait bucket,
wet my hands in it and one by one
let the minnows go.
It is quiet, the water warm.
I think how summer is not quite gone,
of my father each November swearing
he could hear peepers in the Homesville swamp.
I remember my dead friend's letter
from Spain, the large key carried
each day to the room above the rented house,
his small son's fingers red with wine,
the Tarentella danced one evening
against the bite of love or grief.

Later I will tell the woman and child
of floating toward shore,
of how the bow scraped up on gravel,
and the moon a sliver of onion.
How the weeds rustled as I stepped
out of the boat and the killdeer rose
from my feet like things released
and circled above me crying.
How I felt neither unreasonable nor sad
in my fear, and found it possible
in the end to sit and listen,
not seeing the other shore
nor anything more of such dark flying.

Swimming with Foxes

So comes the fox at evening
up from the quarry out of the pines
down the dirt road the mist around him
swirling like small bass in shallows
Comes to the chicken heads we have left
weaves in and out of our eyes
as we sit behind the big window
watching his redness the green of August
his eyes and snout with their long habits
of shyness and mice

When he leaves we walk to the quarry
and swim till midnight The clear water
reminds us of ways of coming up dirt roads
or out of pines or white birches at evening
while all around us from behind
the dark panes of rock and burrow
the fox is watching

On Not Fishing the Brodhead This Year

I am sitting in this red afternoon
considering the shadow along the bone
from my ankle to knee, I am thinking
of sailboats past blue-eyed grass
and young girls in straw hats,
and how I have spent another evening or morning
and overlooked the lightweight graphite rod
and the tan vest with its pockets
of Quill Gordons and Gray Fox Variants.

And how as I am walking out tomorrow
or the next day, I will hear something behind
the yellowhammer's nest, and will stop
and try for balance as though on the Brodhead's
round and slippery rocks, and might wonder
at the leaves moving in the windless day
and the small butterfly suddenly snapped
out of the air.

Though there is only the deep moss
at the foot of the honeysuckle vine,
and the nest shaken loose last night
from the dark slant of the locust
and near it the tiny naked dead.
As it grows cooler, greener,
I will sit here still as a young turtle
beneath the pointed circling wings,
I will not move until dark,
until stars hatch above me thick as damselflies.

The Long Habit of Fire

There's no telling what floats past at midnight
or rises just before dawn and comes ashore.
Even at noon the rocks are darker
than old blood on a sleeve.
And here's where leaves hide something
near the shore, white hands or dead shad.
The water has sad bells in it.

But do not worry for me
even though I am sitting by a blue tent
near the first deep pools of the Scarewater.
I have a map of the tangles of rootends
under the washed-out banks that could catch
a man's legs or belt loops.
And I have learned to freeze
when I hear the clicking like old crockery
and have practiced the handholds of the one trail
up through cribbing and rip-rap.
All afternoon the valley falters,
copperhead ledges grow damp as tide flats.

If someone suddenly turns up,
say wife or daughter or father,
and my words go right through them,
or if I hear my name called out,
I do not look up but pretend there are deerflies
in my eyes, or gather sticks and stones
and think of a bright window with music.

Or close my eyes,
and swaying with the terror of others
remember the long habit of fire,
and sit there waiting for the moon
to come down the riffle in a red canoe.

Building a Tower

for Rachel

Early in spring, probe the air for hints of altitude,
test the ground for skunk cabbage and center of balance,
note the spread of yellow along the finches' wings,
the chilly angles of shagbark and spruce.
When you walk inside to the supper of lentils and hard bread
and the child touches your hand, touch her face and hair,
tell her a story of climbing the blue air like smoke.

At night when you wake to feel the power of roots
through foundation and bed, and your skin burns with dark windows
and the steady flow of landscape, write letters to friends
about wind velocity or the book about Machu Picchu.

One morning at first light, slip out the back door,
stand near the place in your mind where you feel most at home,
study the setting moon, the first clues of sun.
There'll be pine siskin or redpolls at the feeder,
turtle doves fluttering in as you gather boards
from the shed, cans of nails, your father's saw,
and begin to hammer winter out of your skin.

In a week there will be winds over planking,
nails curling like sunspots near your boots.
Occasionally a car will slow or drive past a second time.
The child will eat oranges and think of blue air at her window.

When you see the first vultures of the year or dream of trout
swimming near a neighbor's daughter, walk into the hardwood flats
and build a fire, diagram the sky with your walking stick, drink wine.
Soon you will be free of vultures and dreams of trout.
You will hold your good steel rule to mountains and stars
and be able to name the currents of dark hours passing.

For mornings on end, wonder about the small flashes of pink
on a far-off hill, think of bloodroot and hepatica,
the last arcs of snow against the stream's bank.
Think of falling as the one perfect thing the world does,
the unexpected pleasure of warm wrists, the blood pouring
behind your eyes, light across the spaniel's back,
the solid feel of tools in your tanned hands.

But one afternoon in June, for no reason you can think of,
as pheasants and grouse perch on your ladder and chain saw,
your hands turn up idle and folded in the sun.

Below you, the woman and child gather crawfish and watercress
and you nod toward them, wondering if they remember
lentils and hard bread, the naps you often took on the porch
as dusk came on like swirls of wood grain.
You might call out in a voice that sounds like yarrow,
like softest weather crossing your lips and tongue,
and you will feel like doing something amazing
with yourself, maybe standing on air for once

and not losing your grip.

And so before you lose touch
with moonlight and pine trees, before your hands become red giants,
then dwarfs, then dense magnets, before you forget water,
the sound of names, or how to walk into a room of faces,
begin by pulsebeat by nerve-end
by the slow hand over hand of inches to go back down.

The Man Who Loved Fish

In his house or on his way to work
he sees fields opening and closing like gills,
flashes of soft white bellies
drifting slowly over woodpile and den.
He touches the scaly sides of old barns,
trees like red carp.

In August he dreams of droughts, puddles drying up,
feels the moon's tug, wades through the pools
of his basement where shadows wait like herons,
where things glide past furnace and workbench,
where he mourns the bones of Delaware shad
and catfish washing ashore near his driveway.

Quickly now, before it's too late, look through
this window, notice his wife and children,
the one-eyed cat on the rug.
Notice how the whole room ripples
between end table and magazine rack,
how he slowly rises, turns off the lights.

Can you hear it now? the splashes, the croak of frogs,
soft wings rising, a watersnake sliding from its limb?

Can you believe such love swimming off into the night?

The Man Who Smuggled Life to Work
Day after Day

Every day there were the faces to get past
He knew their names watched their hands
the way they spoke as he passed
Once inside he listened
to a sound like dry sticks between his fingers
or water where a stream forked
and a woman looked for stars
It was the darkness he could feel and embers
the hot syllables hidden in the lining of his coat
and bags of sticks and stones
bones of dead animals sewn to his blood

All day long he crossed the borders of desk
and typewriter address book secretary
It was when the sun briefly fired his clothes
or when his hand trembled with memory
that he fought back panic walked straight through
the faces gathered like backwaters
though he was sure they'd heard
were even then tapping his pulse for wingbeat
or high howling cave

He thought of the woman on her warm rock
He thought of hawkweed and yarrow
At four the faces walked away
He stood near his desk
and pulled bird after bird from a trick in his knee
took from his heel a fire from his sleeve
a great fish a map from under his tongue
opened his coat's lining for the hot syllables
and let all of it loose
                  there in the dusk of the office
filled the air with bloodbeat and earth

Then he walked down the small street
past the windows where the faces still watched

Tomorrow he would palm mountain peaks and rock walls
He would hide spiders and dens in his eyes
On his back behind his knee under his arm
would be the plunging waters the smell of swamp
the woman washing her bright hair

Listening to One Thing at a Time

Say it is evening and a neighbor's hardwoods
float on the mosquito mist rising from the fields,

or morning and a woman in a black dress
sits on a bed twisting her fingers around and around

and talking of white blossoms,
say it is the air picking up speed

and the season unfolding like a shape you almost miss.
Maybe the woman is now by a table

studying the red-winged blackbirds
calling above the hickory and mint.

Say there is a road north with foxglove and lobelia,
that it is only the whistling
behind the crockery of late afternoon
or just before dawn that causes her to pause

and for a moment remember a single sound
like ice sliding into Baffin Bay,

the green note of memory this blue day
singing through a grain of dust.

The Christian Woman and Sasquatch

for—but not about—Mary Ann Waters

You have to say it was something
moved from tree to tree, that stepped
dull-footed on the twig that woke her,
something whose throat had mountain fog in it
and canyons and switchback ridges.

Have to say it was something
lifted the red pack from its tree,
circled fireplace and tent, and shadows
rising and falling, a guy line vibrating
from a touch that chilled her deeper
into chapter and verse of sleeping bag.

Have to say she did hear the tent's zipper
and so sang softly of grace and the salmon
and eagles of Coeur d'Alene,
that she sang to stars or eyes or the yellow teeth
or the smell of fur.

You have to say it was something
she closed her eyes on, that at last withdrew
past boots and up the sheer cliff,
that paused and made one last small sound
like the brush of cold rain over moss,
then seemed to melt or die or else
became the mountain and its hidden lake
or first light finding a lonely place.

To My Brother This Night
on the Delaware River

for William Davis Humes

Long after midnight I'm awake
wondering if you've swamped,
lost everything, the green plastic bags
floating away like bobbers,
and your boat caught
on the undertowed limbs near shore.
Are you like our father at his end,
falling, trying to breathe?
Or are you, brother, this night
saved again as when we stood
all summer long as boys
before the alter of the Methodist Church?

I imagine you safely past Foul Rift,
still in the canoe, still in control,
looking for an island campsite.
My eyes have other rivers in them
through which come other paddlers.
I send them toward you,

and then I sleep and dream
of moonlight over wet rocks,
and you in a blue sleeping bag,
dry as old dawns.

Tomorrow we will meet by the Water Gap.
I will not tell you
of the night of slow tumbling canoes
nor of hands like dead fish
flashing in dark water,
but of blue herons overhead at noon,
the flow of green pools,
the rapids miles behind us,
and the swirl of wooden paddles
blooming around us.

Waiting in the Crow Roost, He Thinks
of the Woman Who Went Back to the City

I have smeared my face and hands with mud
and built a small blind where I wait
for the long line of crows to come
as they do each evening across the valley
like smoke from an old steamer.
It is dusk, clear after weeks of rain.
A small wind comes over the rosehip berries,
as the first of them beat up the hollow
and over the Mennonite Church.
I have been thinking of you in the city,
your books and apricot tea,
that gray light off the river,
and cannot say why I am here again
with thermos and binoculars,
except to watch the limbs bending
beneath the weight of so many crows,
how some tumble past each other,
swooping close above my head,
their open mouths like sleet storms.

Sometimes when they settle for the night,
the rustling over, beaks clicked shut,
I want to climb one of the oaks,
and not worry about my neck or eyes,
that I might rise without their knowing,
to sit there, running my hands
over wingtips and legs, humming a little song.

You would like it now,
the stillness and a dog barking far off,
the way the night so completely happens,
not sad or complicated, but something else,
the piece of wood smooth against my hand,
and farther off than the dogs,
a mountain dulcimer or great owl,
and all of it fitting together,
my hand on the piece of wood,
the stones beneath me grown into the roots,
things edging upward, evenly,
to the point where feathers merge
with the ends of leaves, and beyond.

Once I stayed in this place until dawn,
but that was like going beyond a season.
So in a while I will walk back,
past the stone house
with its broken windows and well sweep,
searching the overgrown garden
for wode or late foxglove,
and then along the trail by the stream,
farther and farther from this dark weather
swaying at the tops of trees.

Gifts by the Edge of the Woods

Last night in the fire
I watched a branch moving
as though it were alive.
It was only a stick burning through,
but for a while I was afraid
of the life of flames, of darkness.

The branch lifted one last time
and I thought of a rattlesnake
I once crippled with a stick
along a mountain trail,
and then to please a girl,
knelt before its flat head
inviting its feeble strike.

Now in this light, I read again
the note my daughter, age ten,
gave me last night before she slept.

All evening she'd been hearing
something I could not,
her frustration bringing her
almost to tears. She tells me
It's all right I could not hear it,
that she thinks it must have been the cicada
rubbing its legs together.
It's all right.

Now I am thinking of forgiveness,
how it comes for years down the seasons
of rain and snow, down perfect blue days,
light sparkling over the grass,
and how it is the oldest of words,
how it was first in the void,
a great river of dust, mountains,
a snake turning over and over
in the dry leaves by a trail,
a girl unbuttoning her blouse.

Before we leave this place,
my daughter and I
will search through our packs
for something small and precious,
we will walk down past the swamp
and up Double Fork Trail
until we come to the edge of the woods
where there is some tansy,
we will leave our gifts there,

and think of cicadas, the curl of fire,
the sorrow of language,
we will remember the small prayers,
say goodbye to the mice and wrens,
we will take a last look around,
a few seconds more.

The Photograph

1.

Maybe it is Easter, 1940
He has my brother in one arm
and me in the other
There are some swings and a pigeon coop
in the background
He has been coughing for days
into his red-flecked handkerchief
and his breathing
sounds like sleet against a window

2.

I think of him folding his napkin neatly
into his lunch pail then rising on thin legs
and walking down a gangway
through the dusty air

3.
Do I hear him now at the front door
then the back Does he climb the side steps
and knock softly on a window

I don't know
In the photograph
he seems like a man thinking of nothing
but holding his two small sons

At the Shad Festival

My father never fished for shad,
but each Good Friday he would leave at noon
and return at dusk with daffodils
for my mother, and stories about men
with nets beneath a river bridge,
and the way his friend boned the shad,
and later the peppery taste of watercress
fresh from the stream behind a springhouse
miles and miles from our house
in the valley of coal mines.

And so I think of him
this half-sunny afternoon
while we wait in line for our paper plates
with their white and brown flesh,
baked potatoes, and mint tea,
of how he's been gone these twenty years
and that it's taken me that long
to understand his solitary trips
to his friend's house to eat shad

and talk of the surge of that great fish
up the channels and pools of the Delaware,
the females circling the gravel bottom.

I think of the way he would walk to his garden
to bury the bones he would carry home,
how he would pat the earth down
between pepper and tomato plants.
And then on Holy Saturday
gather us to his idleness
and take us uptown to the firehouse,
and one by one sit us in the driver's seat
of that great red truck, each of us higher
than we would ever be again.
How for a day his white hands
miraculously circled us, planted in us
a direction we would think half our lives
was none but our own.

The Last Miner Is Found

1.

The others have been carried
through smoke to the surface
the faces waiting
in the blue afternoon
but this one
waits with his back against cribbing
his bare head to his chest

2.

He was the first on the vein's face
the one who saw the timber splitting
or felt the air still
before the tunnel sucked at him
blew his eyes shut
even before he could yell out

He has been sitting there
these three days
like someone waiting
for pigeons to come in at evening

Now he is the last to be wrapped in white
and placed gently in the gunboat
and carried to the small point
of light that falls toward his stiff face
like the cruelest of cave-ins.

White Birch Father

I drive the narrow road to Packer Number Five
and stop by the concrete slab
that now covers the mine head.
Beneath it the tunnels have caved in
or filled with water.
All around me on the dark ground
are pieces of splintery wood from office
or breaker or maybe the washroom
where the men lifted their clothes
and mining gear along a string to the ceiling.
Here and there lie rusted strands
of the steel cable
that lowered them 1200 feet in cages
and hauled them up a shift later.
I think of the light from their lamps
slithering down the timbered pit,
of mules and sirens at night,
last messages scratched in leather belts,
of the summer my brother and I,

eight and ten, stepped up
to the visiting evangelist to be saved.

White birch rustle around me
and heat waves blur the hills and slag banks,
as I walk up to where the fan house
used to be, then higher,
to the escape tunnel a mile
from the main shaft, and see my father
crawling from it in 1946 and 1950.
There are beams across it now,
and I put my face next to them,
to the smell of slate and soggy dark.
I go farther, following a small stream
of orange and bitter water,
to a place that falls sharply away,
sides jagged as bad weather.
I drop a rock and think of the stories
of sinkholes appearing overnight
by a back porch, the slow tilting of a house,
the swimming hole and the boy in it
sucked down. In this country of caves,
I sit on a stump and remember
my one-armed grandfather who wore a hook
he'd strap on like a gangster's rig
and use to hoe his garden.
Or hear again my father telling
about watching the rats,
how they were always the first to hear
the cracks beginning in timber or rock.

It is mid-afternoon as I walk back
past snakeroot and dog fennel to the slab.
There is no date on it,
no names of those still down there
reaching for lunch bucket or trying to run,
no mention of my father
in his white summer clothes,
nor the first red flecks in his spit,
the erosion of his breath,
no mention of the high room
in which one spring he died.

I drive down into the town
with its rows of houses like drab teeth
set too close together, to the one house
with its red shingles and single gable.
As I enter, it is the silence
that is most familiar, the lonesome smell
as though a good lake had gone dry
and left behind wooden table,
neatly tied packets of *Upper Rooms,*
the cups from Nova Scotia and Spain.
I pick up the Methodist hymnal
and sit by the east window and wonder
what my father saw when he sat
looking off into the hills on which
the birch had not yet arrived.
I look into the corner and see
the black Queen Bengel coal stove
with its silver oven plate,
then down into the garden

where I imagine him holding up
for the camera a litter of beagle pups
and whistling "Rock of Ages."

But it is the cellar I want,
where it is like putting my face
against the bars of the escape tunnel.
I stop at the spot where in 1919
a man shot and killed
my father's sister and then himself.
This is where I peeled the skins
from muskrat and fox,
pulled them like gloves
over boards to dry,
this is where my mother came to cry,
and where my father kept his tools.
They are what I have come for,
and I place them along one wall,
long and short augers, cross cut,
the bull jack and sledgehammer.
I sit there a while longer,
touching them one by one,
thinking how I will carry them upstairs
and out to my car, and how they will rattle
on the seat beside me,
giving off their small storms of dust.

Mountain Lake with Stumps

There's more to it than driving a road
and seeing the stumps like dark pins in a map,
and then the way I stop and walk out
to the wooden boat rotting on its chain.
More to it than the horseshoe sunk in clay
and the way suddenly I want to hear something
over the water, to have its great fish
swim close to shore, more than how I want to be out there
by the stumps with the light on me like bark,
and peeling it back to find a message
about hard weather or love,
or what happened one soft evening in a back cove,
a man and a boy fishing,
and then a woman on shore waving them in.
And later by a dark window the smell of wild chives,
a single splash out on the water.

One Approach to the Steppes

It may be I have been too long studying
the place on the ridge the moon will touch first,
or too long considering the power
of ice through walls and pipes and sleep,
or the gray cat curled up all day and night
with something in his blood.
Or that I stood too long last October
in the abandoned house with its beer cans,
scorched mattress, smashed walls.
                              Perhaps
it is only the quail calling in the old orchard
and circling against more powerful weathers
than these that make me think of icons
and snarling dogs, girls with high dark cheeks
and bright scarves, or a man in long coat
and hat flying above a red and blue domed church.

I walk past the overturned canoe
with him on my mind, with what rattles
in the weeds and bare limbs of the trees,
or goes on inside them, inside the white hives
on the hillside, the wet ends of things waiting.
Then I enter the small house
beneath the locust trees, carrying with me
a piece of wood. It is shaped like a bird.
Look, I say to the woman weaving yarrow
and lavender and hyssop into small wreaths.

Look.

Ridge Music

In this place above the frozen lake,
these woods halfway up the Blue Mountain,
it must have happened for seasons
of sad air across ax-head and wagon,
must have been a long walk to the springhouse
or through the dozen rows of fir trees
or around the half-mile of stone fence.

Where weather by weather maybe they began
to look past each other, having heard something
first faintly high on the ridge like the whisper
of owls mating in January, or lower down
the booming woodpeckers all through March,
till one night in the kerosene glow they looked up
and heard it closer, just beyond the door,
and huddled together and did not sleep,
thinking all night of that place in the root cellar
for whatever went wrong, that had to wait for spring.

Where by morning there was nothing
beyond the door, though it had happened,
though they stood all morning by corn plants
and beans and put their hands on the shining trail,
though they watched all summer and fall,
sat long winter nights listening,
though there was nothing ever again.

Here by these old foundations and caved-in fence,
I think of zinc-lidded jars of basil and sage
on shelves above the black stove
with its bright oven plate,
or boots and woolen shirts, dark hats,
the blue linen dress in its box,
and children climbing into the high loft.
Or of fevers, night cries, dawn terror and ice
in this place where now it has begun to snow,
and wind to claw down face and neck.
I put my hand on pieces of glass, frozen moss,
touch the old tree's initials
that have drifted out beyond recognition.
It is like an insect's cold blood, this afternoon
around me, as I imagine failure of logs
and fire, music over the ridge.

Improvements on Empty Space

What's left of the day
comes slant to the back of my hand
like Brueghel's hunters
through the snow, some peasants
behind them singeing a pig.

I think of Einstein
stepping off his trolley
beneath the tower clock in Berne.
I wonder how deep the blacksnake lies
beneath the foundation of my house,
and want to see the woman
in a blue summer dress.

Listen, it is the only way
I can see the world at such speed as this,
the only way I know how to behave
at such an hour, my neighbor's horse
down off the hillside,
the bamboo rake thrown down
near the pile of yellow leaves.

Bee Hive in Early December

As I could not do all summer long
I walk close enough to touch it humming
in wind like some deep season's buoy,
and remember an afternoon I watched
the steady lines in and out for hours.
Now I would like to take it all apart
and pile it piece by piece near the stone fence,
discover dry thorax and eye, torn wings,
summer's small failures.

I look toward Ziegel's Church,
at the Mennonite's wagon, his horse
steaming, red wheels redder against the afternoon.

Last night it was a neighbor at my door
with venison, news of his wife,
of wells going cloudy or dry. Here by ice
and a fog drifting down from the high woods
I would like to take the season apart
hill by hill, well by well, darkness by darkness,

to touch warm eyes of mud wasp,
sleep heave of beasts, centers of birch or oak,
the ancient slime.

I turn from the hive
and walk past dry pennyroyal and bittersweet,
down the path toward the springhouse.
First flakes fall randomly,
chicadees move from branch to branch.
Far off, near the cider maker's house,
there's shouting, a door opening and closing,
an unexpected arrival.

Caught in the Woods in the Dark

Sometimes in November
I sit too long by the initials
someone carved in the oak tree
thirty years before,
and then the dark comes up
out of the leaves and grapevines,
up along my legs and shoulders,
and my eyes go dry with the crunch
of leaves and whisper of owls.
Once in a while in such dark,
I grow afraid to turn my head
for fear something will be there,
though I know there will be nothing
making itself solid out of wind,
that it is not breathing I hear
behind me all the way to the stream,
and half across the soybean field,
where in the sudden relief of the middle,

it is like being in the old family De Soto,
and the years of the dark changed,
as though something
had pulled itself up and over my head,
as though the rest of the way back
I were a child asleep
during a long drive from the sea.

Winter Storm Watch

In this afternoon of dark December
coming too quickly past the blaze-orange coats
of hunters, I watch first flakes of a storm
that's tracked us for days. Vivaldi
the one-eyed cat moves past table and rocker
like a last measure; my small daughter
breathes easily, safely through her nap.

It is almost like old crockery,
the light that slips behind locust and holly.
Pheasants flare briefly in the orchard,
snow begins to hiss and smolder
across winter wheat.

The shadows in this room remind me
of places where something has drifted
too sweetly from face to face,
or of how I have often waked before dawn
for no good reason and wandered
from bedroom to kitchen,

listening to walls and water pipes,
and then, still restless, gone back to bed
to dream of women in linen blouses.

Everywhere now, by rose-hip berries
and frozen stream, silence gathers.
By morning it will be whiter,
deeper, called a single name.

The Snow Snake

I walk to the orchard,
the frozen pond, and there
by a stump, half-coiled and smooth,

its eyes like dark places
inside a stream, the snake.
I think of my father's father

saying they never den,
not these white ones,
and all winter drift higher

toward pheasants at roost,
or past the yellow stalks
of nightshade. Now it yawns

into the curve of sky,
rubs its diamond head
along a snag of root,

catches part of its mouth,
and slowly begins to work,
taking its muscular time

through the opal dusk
until it is free. I watch
a small bird eat red berries,

and remember the twine of veins
on the backs of my grandfather's hands,
the sound of his gravelly voice

calling me up to the porch
with its wooden swing and bench,
evenings, his arm around me.

Now I kneel by the root and touch
what has been left behind,
what is sifting over my hand,

and down by the frozen pond,
and past the muskrat's den,
the voice I recognize,

the way it always begins.

The Sermon Stump

I come to the stump in the middle of snow.
All around me old apple trees lean
to the slow hour of words
through this morning's vestibule.
I catch the familiar odor of parents,
neighbors, young girls adrift in choirs.
Pheasants under a thorn bush feed
on the remains of seed and berry.
I speak toward windows and rooms of faces.
There are cats prowling the leaden fields.
I touch children rising like hymns.
Whatever I know of burning is here,
caught in this log's swirling gospel.
Just yesterday there were softer winds,
a migration buoyant with wings.
Now that the winter solstice unnerves us
with its benediction of empty places,
I think of the white whale's rage

against the desolate belly of the world.
The day begins to blur, the year turns gray.
The pond is secret as a prayer closet.
A sudden rush and the last word is out
and it is ghostly in the deep snow
as I turn toward home, flesh aching with limits
and the host of loss singing everywhere.

Calling in the Hawk

I should have a dead mouse in my hands
on this the last day of the year,
and a leather guard the length of my forearm,
for out there on the field's only hickory
is the hawk with its white breast feathers
and its eyes hooking late morning light.
I walk into the field, give out the high whistle,
again and yet again till it shifts on the limb,
one shoulder moving slightly up, one foot restless,
the head looking away, looking back.

Then it drops off, comes low over dry grass
and old barley, flaps slowly, powerfully over briars.
I whistle again. It grows larger,
sets its wings. I raise my right arm.
I see the flaring red tail, the way
feathers hold air like fingers over a balloon,
and there are the nostril slits, the curved beak,
wings tilted, braking, talons tearing
into my arm. It sits there, waiting.

I whisper *pheasant* to it. It leaves my arm,
rises next to clouds, stoops over the orchard,
again comes back low, a great red cock
trailing beneath it, comes whish to my arm.
I take the pheasant, cook it with wild rice.
The hawk waits someplace else. After wine
I whistle. It comes down through the maples,
lands on the porch. I call it to my bleeding arm.
Good bird, I say, as my dog watches.
Showing off for the woman, I whisper *blue jay*.
It spirals off, comes back. I offer blue
tail feathers for her to weave into the raffia
basket, to wear in her hair, to put in a vase.
She refuses.
                    I am careful not to whisper
fire or *serpent* or *fox-trap*, not to whisper
sunspots or *meteor*, *the depressing distances*
of space. It sits on the scars of my arm
for years. It is pleased I haven't ordered
jess and hood, as it stretches its wings
of February nights. I signal *no*,
that this is the month of sorrow, of dangerous
air heaves, the sink holes by the stream.
The woman piles her baskets in the pantry.
She grows fat, looks at me with distrust,
refuses to pet the bird. One day in March
its head drops, it begins to sleep past noon,
curls up on my arm. The vet thinks accipitor
leukemia, no cure, better to put it down.
So the leg is shaved, the needle inserted.
Outside near the shovel, I whisper, *It happens*.

The next day it is back with something black
happening in its talons, wants to land on my arm.
No, I shout, *Take it back.* I run inside,
hide behind the woman who nurses her child.
It circles the house for days.
I call out *skunk cabbage, spring peeper,*
bloodroot, hepatica. It circles and circles,
talons locked, eyes blazing with friendship.
Through my cupped hands I yell *trout,*
long walks, warm rain, the woman naked on the grass.
It circles the red roof, the grackles building nests.
At last I walk out. It is June, the air
buoyant with thermals. I whistle it down
through the air. It is all familiar.
All afternoon and evening it approaches.
Deep down in my blood something begins.
The final word flaps closer and closer.